D1587758

STUPENDOUS AND TREMENDOUS SCIENCE

SPECTACULAR (AND SOARING) SPACE

ENTER A UNIVERSE OF STARTLING STARS!

Claudia Martin

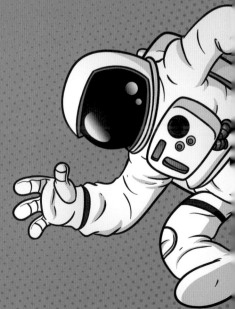

WAYLAND

First published in Great Britain in 2022 by Wayland

Copyright © Hodder and Stoughton Limited, 2022

Produced for Wayland by
White-Thomson Publishing Ltd
www.wtpub.co.uk

Author and editor: Claudia Martin
Series Designer: Rocket Design (East Anglia) Ltd
Illustrator: Steve Evans
Proofreader: Annabel Savery

HB ISBN: 978 1 5263 1610 3
PB ISBN: 978 1 5263 1623 3

Wayland
An imprint of
Hachette Children's Group
Part of Hodder & Stoughton
Carmelite House
50 Victoria Embankment
London EC4Y 0DZ

An Hachette UK Company
www.hachette.co.uk
www.hachettechildrens.co.uk

Printed in China

Illustrations by Steve Evans: 3tr, 3br, 4, 5c, 7b, 8b, 9b, 14c, 16, 18cr, 19tr, 20, 25c, 26b, 28br, 29tr, 29br.

Picture acknowledgements: iStock: MarcelC 13c, oversnap 13cr; Getty Images: Digital Vision 13cl; NASA: Jet Propulsion Lab 17tl, JPL/Caltech 21br, Endeavour 24br, CXC/NGST 27cr; Shutterstock: Fun Way Illustration front cover br, MemoAngeles front cover br, 1br, 31cr, Blue Ring Media front cover bg, Oceloti front cover bl, yusufdemirci front cover tr, back cover, Tartila 1tr, 1bl, 10–11, 30, 31, Ivan Nikulin 2, 11br, Jemastock 3tl, 3cr, 3bl, 5tl, Sakurra 6bl, GraphicSurfCom 7tr, Lorelyn Medina 9t, Natali Snailcat 12, 6x6x6 13tr, mr.Timmi 14bc, 15bl, Whitelion61 14br, NoPainNoGain 15tr, Tristan3D 15bc, NASA/Dotted Yeti 17bl, 27bl, NASA/Digital Images Studio 18–19, Meowu 21c, NASA/Aphelleon 21bl, NASA Images 22cl, 22cr, 22bl, Gtspace 22br, delcarmat 23tr, 3Dsculptor 25bl, klyaksun 26b/bg, Juergen Faelchle 27cl, Vadim Sadovski 27c; Smithsonian Institution @ Flickr Commons: 23br. All additional design elements from Shutterstock or drawn by designer.

SPECTACULAR AND SOARING CONTENTS

YOUR UNIVERSE

You live on a planet that is warmed by a star called the Sun. Our planet is one of at least 100 billion planets in a galaxy called the Milky Way. Scientists estimate that there are up to 2 trillion galaxies in the universe.

HOW BIG IS THE UNIVERSE?

The universe that we can see from Earth is huge: 93 billion light years across. A single light year is the distance that light travels in a year: 9.46 trillion km (5.88 trillion miles). The universe has not always been so big. Most scientists think that, 13.8 billion years ago, the universe started to grow from a tiny point. This idea is called the Big Bang theory.

HOW big is it?! I think I need a longer ruler.

IS THERE EMPTY SPACE IN ... SPACE?

In a galaxy, the space between stars is not empty: it contains gas and dust. Galaxies are usually at least 3 million light years apart: that space between galaxies is much emptier. There may be one atom of gas in each 1 cubic metre (35 cubic feet) of space. An atom is a particle so small that it cannot be seen by human eyes.

Everything from people to stars is made of atoms. Trillions of atoms could fit on to one full stop.

Pwwwww

IS THE UNIVERSE GROWING?

Astronomers can see that other galaxies are moving away from us. This tells us that the universe is expanding. Galaxies are like spots drawn on to a balloon that is being blown up. As the balloon inflates, the space between the spots gets bigger!

FREAKY FACT

We are used to measuring objects in three dimensions: length, width and height. Scientists say that the universe has a fourth dimension – time. Even more mind-bendingly, it may have many other dimensions that we cannot see or experience.

5

EXTRAORDINARY EARTH

Earth is one of eight planets in our solar system, all of them moving in roughly circular paths, called orbits, around the Sun. The solar system is all the planets and smaller objects that orbit the Sun.

WHAT IS EARTH MADE OF?

Earth formed around 4.5 billion years ago in a cloud of gas and dust spinning around the newborn Sun. The gas and dust clumped together, making super-hot spinning balls that became planets. The inner planets – Mercury, Venus, Earth and Mars – are made of heavy materials. The larger, outer planets – Jupiter, Saturn, Uranus and Neptune – are made of lighter materials that were blown away from the Sun. Earth's heaviest materials sank to its core, which is made of hot metal, mostly iron and nickel. Earth's cooler, outer layers are rocky.

Earth has been cooling since it formed, but the core is still 6,000 °C (10,800 °F).

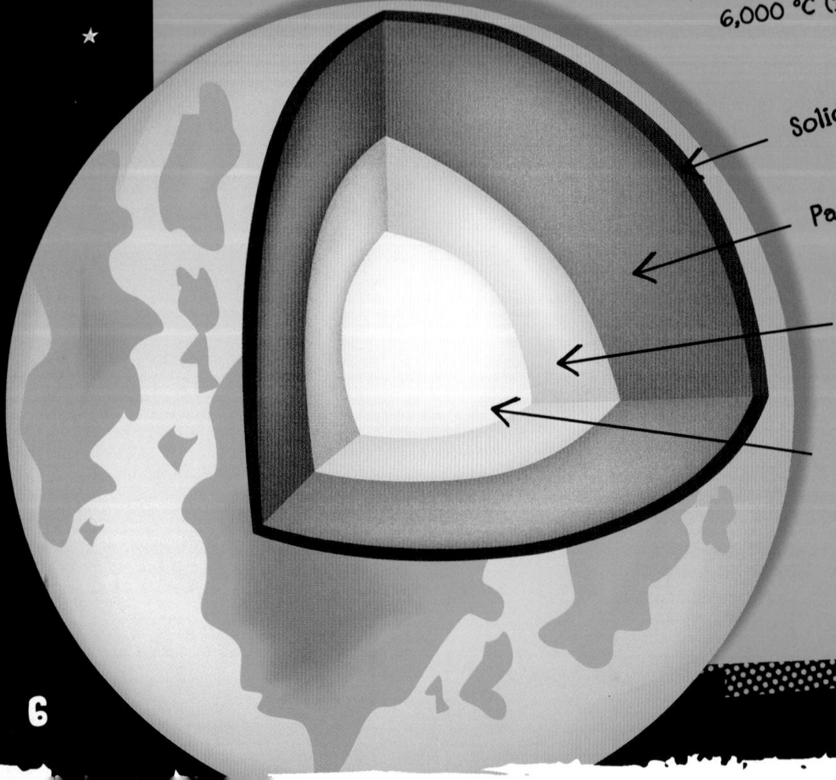

Solid rock crust

Partly melted rock mantle

Liquid metal outer core

Solid metal inner core

WHAT STOPS EARTH FROM SHOOTING OFF INTO SPACE?

Earth is held in orbit by the Sun's gravity. Gravity is a force that pulls all objects towards each other. The more massive the object, the stronger the pull of its gravity. Earth's gravity stops humans from falling off the planet! Since the Sun is the most massive object in the solar system, its gravity keeps the planets moving around it, in anticlockwise orbits.

WHERE DOES SPACE BEGIN?

Earth's gravity holds a mixture of gases, called air, around it. This blanket of air is called the atmosphere. It contains nitrogen, oxygen, carbon dioxide and other gases. Oxygen is needed by animals to breathe. The atmosphere also traps enough heat from the Sun to keep us warm. There is no definite line between the atmosphere and space. Gases are pulled weakly by Earth's gravity as far as 10,000 km (6,200 miles) above Earth's surface. Yet when we talk about a rocket entering space, we normally mean it has flown higher than 100 km (62 miles).

BOUNCE!

CRASH!

What about gravity!!!

Mmmmm, just right!

SUPER SCIENCE

Astronomers say Earth is in the 'Goldilocks zone'. In the fairy tale, Goldilocks turned down porridge that was either too hot or too cold, choosing the bowl that was just right! Earth is at the right distance from the Sun for it to be neither so hot that all water boils away into steam, nor so cold that all water freezes into ice. Earth is warm enough for water to flow to water plants and to drink, making life possible.

MARVELLOUS MOON

Earth is not on its own: it has a constant companion, the Moon, which orbits our planet at an average distance of 384,402 km (238,856 miles). A moon is a large, rounded object that orbits a larger planet.

WHAT HAPPENED TO THE PLANET 'THEIA'?

Many astronomers think the Moon formed after a space crash! The crash may have happened soon after Earth formed, when our planet was still very hot. A Mars-sized planet, which astronomers call Theia, may have crashed into Earth. The crash sent rubble shooting into space, where its own gravity pulled it into a ball: the Moon. Earth's stronger gravity kept the Moon in orbit around our planet.

A young Earth

Out of the waaaay!

Move left!

Theia

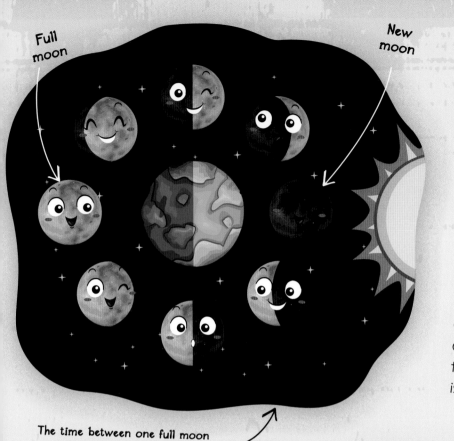

Full moon

New moon

The time between one full moon and the next is 29.5 days.

WHY DOES THE MOON SEEM TO CHANGE SHAPE?

We can see the Moon because the Sun's light shines on it. The Sun always lights up the side of the Moon that is facing the Sun. As the Moon travels around Earth, we see more or less of the Moon's lit side. When the Moon passes between the Sun and Earth, we cannot see the lit side. This is called a 'new moon'. When the Moon is on the opposite side of Earth from the Sun, we see the whole lit side. This is called a 'full moon'.

 FACT

Only 12 humans have ever walked on the Moon. The first was US astronaut Neil Armstrong, swiftly followed by Buzz Aldrin, who both set foot on its surface on 21 July 1969.

WHAT ARE THE MOON'S SEAS MADE OF?

The Moon has a metal core and a rocky mantle and crust. The crust is marked by dips called impact craters where it was hit by flying space rocks. The dark areas we can see from Earth are called 'seas' because people used to think they were filled with water. In fact, these dark patches were made when ancient volcanoes erupted, spilling molten rock onto the surface. When this rock cooled, it was darker than the rest.

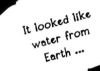
It looked like water from Earth ...

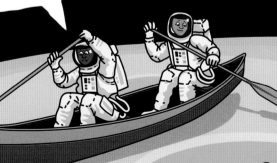

ROCKY PLANETS

The solar system's inner planets – Mercury, Venus, Earth and Mars – have metal cores and rocky mantles and crusts. They are often called terrestrial (or 'Earth-like') planets, but none of the others is suitable for life ... right now.

WHY IS VENUS POISONOUS?

Venus has a thick atmosphere, but it is very different from Earth's. It is mostly carbon dioxide, a gas that in such large quantities would be poisonous to humans. The carbon dioxide traps the Sun's heat, giving Venus an average surface temperature of 460 °C (860 °F), which is hot enough to melt metals such as lead.

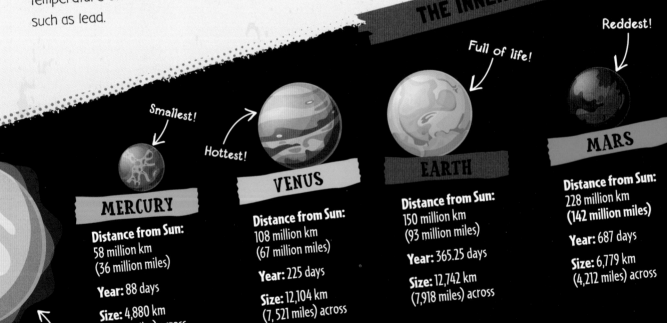

THE INNER PLANETS

Reddest!

Full of life!

Smallest!

Hottest!

MERCURY

Distance from Sun:
58 million km
(36 million miles)

Year: 88 days

Size: 4,880 km
(3,032 miles) across

VENUS

Distance from Sun:
108 million km
(67 million miles)

Year: 225 days

Size: 12,104 km
(7,521 miles) across

EARTH

Distance from Sun:
150 million km
(93 million miles)

Year: 365.25 days

Size: 12,742 km
(7,918 miles) across

MARS

Distance from Sun:
228 million km
(142 million miles)

Year: 687 days

Size: 6,779 km
(4,212 miles) across

SUN

HOW LONG IS A YEAR ON MERCURY?

On any planet, a year is the time taken to make one orbit of the Sun. On Earth, that is 365.25 days. Since this is an awkward number for calendars, we count a year as 365 days, but every four years we have a leap year with an extra day. On Mercury, a year lasts around 88 Earth days. As the closest planet to the Sun, Mercury has the shortest orbit and the shortest year.

·FReAKY· FACT

Like all the planets, Venus also rotates as it travels around the Sun. The time it takes a planet to rotate is the length of its day (from sunrise to sunrise). It takes Venus 243 Earth days to rotate once, giving it the longest day of any solar system planet. Its day is longer than its year!

THE OUTER PLANETS

Not all the planets in the solar system are rocky. See pages 14–17 for more on the outer planets.

Largest!

Most moons!

Coldest!

Windiest!

NEPTUNE

Distance from Sun:
4.5 billion km
(2.8 billion miles)

Year: 165 years

Size: 49,528 km
(30,775 miles) across

URANUS

Distance from Sun:
2.9 billion km
(1.8 billion miles)

Year: 84 years

Size: 51,118 km
(31,763 miles) across

SATURN

Distance from Sun:
1.4 billion km
(890 million miles)

Year: 29.5 years

Size: 120,536 km
(74,898 miles) across

JUPITER

Distance from Sun:
779 million km
(484 million miles)

Year: 12 years

Size: 142,984 km
(88,846 miles) across

> My problem is I don't really believe in myself.

IS THERE LIFE ON MARS?

There is currently no life on Mars. Life as we know it is not possible without flowing water. Mars's reddish rocky surface is dry and dusty, although there is ice at the poles. However, astronomers think that Mars once had oceans, with waves that left their mark on the planet by wearing away the rocks. Simple life forms might have lived in these oceans, but no evidence of life has yet been found.

WATCH OUT!

As well as the planets and their moons, the solar system contains many smaller rocky, metal and icy objects. These include asteroids, comets and meteoroids. Keep your eyes open! One may come whizzing by ...

ARE ASTEROIDS DANGEROUS?

Asteroids are rocky or metal objects between 1 m (3.3 ft) and almost 1,000 km (620 miles) wide. Most of the solar system's millions of asteroids are orbiting the Sun in the Asteroid Belt, which lies between Mars and Jupiter. However, some have orbits that take them near Earth. Occasionally, a small asteroid hits Earth but does little damage. Astronomers tell us there are no large asteroids heading our way. Unluckily for the dinosaurs, a large asteroid did hit Earth 66 million years ago. Most scientists believe the crash filled the sky with sunlight-blocking dust, which caused most plants to die. In turn, this led to the extinction of the dinosaurs.

No, I don't think that looks dangerous ...

WHY DO COMETS KEEP COMING BACK?

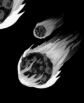

Comets are icy objects with orbits around the Sun that are extremely elliptical (very stretched-out ovals). This means they travel both very close to and far from the Sun. When they near the Sun, they heat up and release gases, so we can see them as bright lights in the sky. The comets with the shortest orbits can be seen every 3 years or so from Earth, while those with the longest orbits may not be seen for 500,000 years.

SEE YOU LATER!

Name: Comet Halley

Orbit length: 75-76 years

Last seen: 1986

SEE YOU ... MUCH LATER!

Name: Comet Hale-Bopp

Orbit length: 2,520-2,533 years

Last seen: 1997

BYEEE!

Name: Comet Neowise

Orbit length: 4,400-6,700 years

Last seen: 2020

HOW MANY METEORITES HIT EARTH EVERY DAY?

A meteorite is a piece of asteroid, comet or meteoroid (a space object smaller than 1 m/3.3 ft across) that lands on Earth's surface. Most objects that enter Earth's atmosphere are burned up by friction (rubbing against the air) as they fall. We see them as bright streaks called shooting stars or meteors. On average, every day fewer than 20 tiny meteorites survive long enough to reach the ground, most of them in deserts or oceans far from people.

SUPER SCIENCE

Just in case a large asteroid does approach Earth, scientists are working on a project called AIDA (Asteroid Impact and Deflection Assessment). They are using their knowledge of forces and motion to work out how to fly an uncrewed spacecraft into an asteroid to send it shooting off in a safer direction.

GASSY AND GIANT

The fifth and sixth planets from the Sun are Jupiter and Saturn. They are called gas giants, but they are not really gassy! They get the name because they are mostly hydrogen and helium, which are gases at the temperatures normally found on Earth.

CAN YOU STAND ON A GAS GIANT?

A gas giant does not have a solid surface, so you would have a hard time standing on one! There is not even a definite dividing line between where the planet ends and the atmosphere begins, although at some point the swirling gas of the atmosphere merges into the swirling liquid of the planet.

Touchdown ... ummm ... touchdown?

WHICH IS THE BIGGEST MOON IN THE SOLAR SYSTEM?

Mercury and Venus don't have moons, but the other six planets in the solar system do. Earth has one while Mars has two, while the outer planets have many more: Jupiter has 79 known moons, Saturn 82, Uranus 27 and Neptune 14. The largest of these moons is Jupiter's Ganymede, which is bigger than the planet Mercury.

WATERY WORLD

1ST PRIZE

Oceans may lie beneath the icy surface.

Name: Ganymede

Orbits planet: Jupiter

Size: 5,268 km (3,273 miles) across

AMAZING ATMOSPHERE

2ND PRIZE

Unusually for a moon, it has a thick atmosphere.

Name: Titan

Orbits planet: Saturn

Size: 5,149 km (3,200 miles) across

WHAT ARE SATURN'S RINGS MADE OF?

Saturn's rings are made of billions of chunks of ice and rock. These chunks are orbiting around the planet's equator. The rings may have formed when one of the planet's moons was smashed to pieces by an asteroid. All four of the outer planets have rings, but Saturn's are the biggest and brightest.

Rings of ice and rock

Gassy hydrogen and helium

Liquid hydrogen and helium

Flowing, metal-like hydrogen

Rock and metal core

Saturn's rings stretch for 400,000 km (250,000 miles) from the planet's surface.

CRAZILY CRATERED

3RD PRIZE

Its surface is completely covered by impact craters.

Name: Callisto

Orbits planet: Jupiter

Size: 4,821 km (2,995 miles) across

VICIOUSLY VOLCANIC

4TH PRIZE

This moon has over 400 active volcanoes.

Name: Io

Orbits planet: Jupiter

Size: 3,660 km (2,274 miles) across

FREAKY FACT

Jupiter has the solar system's longest-lasting storm, which astronomers believe has been raging for at least 350 years. The storm is called the Great Red Spot and can be seen through powerful telescopes as an oval of orange cloud.

ICY AND GIANT

Smaller than the gas giants, Uranus and Neptune are called ice giants. Confusingly, they are not made of ice. They are mostly liquid and gas! But these planets contain lots of materials that scientists call 'ices': water, ammonia and methane.

WHY DOES URANUS ORBIT ON ITS SIDE?

While all the planets are on a bit of a tilt, Uranus is tilted right over, so its axis (an invisible line through its poles) is pointing towards the Sun. The planet seems to roll round the Sun like a ball! Astronomers think this strange tilt may have been caused when another planet crashed into Uranus soon after it formed.

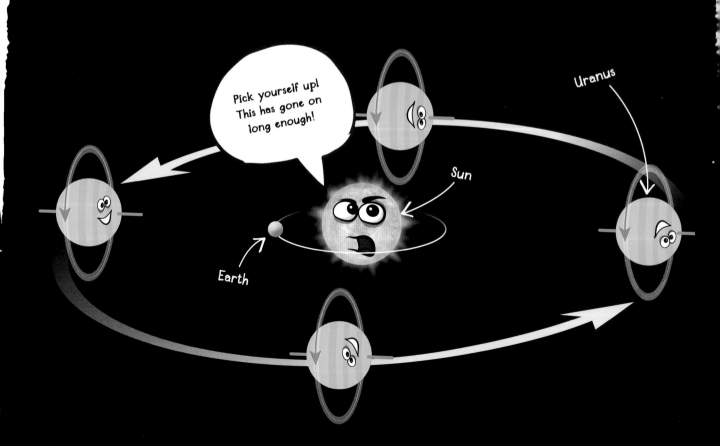

Pick yourself up! This has gone on long enough!

Sun

Earth

Uranus

HOW FAST ARE WINDS ON NEPTUNE?

Neptune has the fastest winds in the solar system, blowing at over 1,770 km (1,100 miles) per hour. Large storms look like dark patches in Neptune's blue atmosphere. It is the methane gas in Neptune's atmosphere that makes the planet look blue. This gas absorbs red light, leaving light that our eyes see as blue. White clouds of frozen methane crystals can be seen around Neptune's storms. These clouds look similar to Earth's high wispy clouds of frozen water crystals.

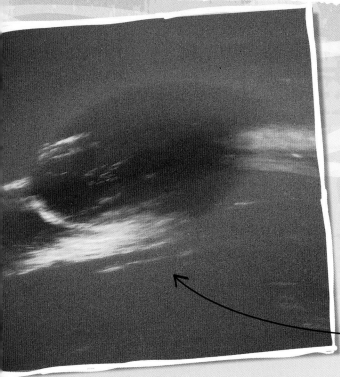

This storm on Neptune was photographed by the Voyager 2 space probe.

WHERE ARE THE DWARF PLANETS?

In addition to the eight planets (or possibly nine; see 'Super Science'), the solar system has at least five dwarf planets. The dwarf planet Ceres is the largest asteroid in the Asteroid Belt (see page 12). Pluto, Makemake, Haumea and Eris lie beyond Neptune, although Pluto's elliptical orbit sometimes takes it closer to the Sun than Neptune. Dwarf planets are smaller than planets. Astronomers define them as being big enough for their own gravity to pull them into a ball shape, but not big enough to clear other large objects out of their region of space.

I've been waiting for someone to notice me for 4.5 billion years.

SUPER SCIENCE

Some astronomers think the solar system has a ninth large planet. If the planet exists, it orbits the Sun at a distance of 60 to 120 billion km (37 to 75 billion miles), far beyond Neptune. Although Planet Nine has never been seen, astronomers believe it may exist because they think that the pull of its gravity is disturbing the orbits of icy objects they are watching in the far solar system.

The largest dwarf planet, Pluto, is 2,376 km (1,476 miles) across.

I'm too small to be a planet, but I am still pretty big!

SUPER SUN

At 1.39 million km (864,938 miles) across, the Sun is a medium-sized star. Like any star, it is a shining ball of super-hot gas – largely hydrogen and helium. The Sun's light takes 8 minutes to travel through space to Earth.

WHY IS THE SUN HOT?

The core of the Sun is 15 million °C (27 million °F). Like all stars, the Sun is hot because atoms of hydrogen are crashing together in its core. The atoms fuse together to become a different type of atom: helium. As they join, they release energy, which we can see and feel millions of kilometres away as light and heat.

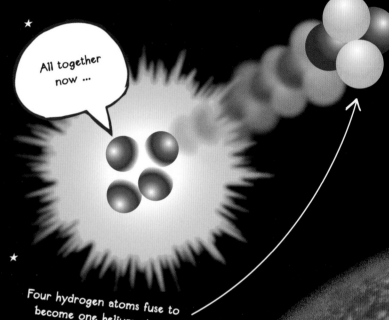

All together now ...

Four hydrogen atoms fuse to become one helium atom.

HOW WAS THE SUN BORN?

The Sun was born around 4.57 billion years ago in a thick cloud of dust and gas. A clump in the cloud grew bigger and bigger, its gravity pulling more and more material towards it. Eventually, the ball of material was overwhelmed by its own gravity and collapsed in on itself. This made it so very, very hot that hydrogen atoms started to crash together. And our star was born!

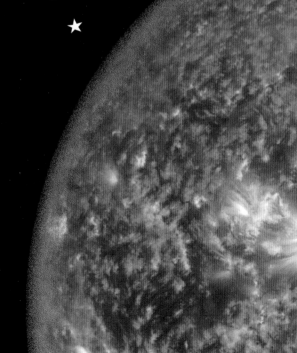

Astronomers created this photo of the Sun using special telescopes and instruments, but we should never look straight at the Sun itself, as its brightness will damage our eyes.

WILL THE SUN DIE?

Like every star, the Sun will die. Luckily for us, our star will not die for another 5 billion years. Around that time, it will run out of hydrogen to use as fuel. It will swell up into what astronomers call a red giant, destroying Mercury, Venus and possibly Earth. For a few million more years, the dying Sun will use its helium as fuel. Then it will shrink into a white dwarf, around the size of Earth. Slowly, it will fade into a dead, cold black dwarf. Stars bigger than the Sun die in an even more dramatic way (see page 20).

Ooof! Is it me or is it getting a bit hot?

FREAKY FACT

A million Earths could fit inside the Sun, but the biggest stars in the universe are around 1,700 times the size of the Sun.

SPARKLING STARS

The universe has at least 1 septillion stars – that is a 1 followed by 24 zeros. The most massive stars usually shine very bright, with their light looking blue to human eyes. Smaller stars may shine yellow or red.

Pssst, Andromeda! Have you heard what Phoenix is up to?

PEGASUS

ANDROMEDA

WHAT ARE CONSTELLATIONS?

Constellations are groups of stars that seem to form the shape of an animal, person or object in the night sky. The stars in a constellation can be millions of kilometres apart, but look close together when viewed from Earth. There are 88 official constellations. The ancient Greeks named 48 of them after people and animals from their myths, such as Pegasus the winged horse. More recently named constellations, such as Microscopium and Telescopium, were often named after scientific instruments.

WHY DO STARS EXPLODE?

When a huge star – at least five times the mass (or weight) of our Sun – runs out of fuel, it explodes in an event called a supernova. The explosion gives off as much light as billions of stars. A supernova leaves behind a tightly packed core of material, called a neutron star; or, for the very biggest stars, a black hole. A black hole is a region of space so tightly packed with material that its gravity is immense. As we know, the more massive the object, the greater the pull of its gravity. Nothing, not even light, can escape the pull of a black hole.

DO OTHER STARS HAVE PLANETS ORBITING THEM?

Until 1992, astronomers did not know of any star other than the Sun that had planets in orbit around it. Then the first exoplanet was found. An exoplanet is a planet outside our solar system. Today, we know of over 3,000 stars with exoplanets. Astronomers have counted over 4,000 exoplanets so far.

The star Trappist 1 holds seven exoplanets in orbit around it.

There are plenty more like me!

SUPER SCIENCE

Exoplanets are too far away to be seen clearly, but astronomers study them for signs they could be habitable (suitable for life). They work out what the temperature and atmosphere of the planet might be like. They also use knowledge gained from other branches of science, such as biology, the study of how plants and animals live on Earth.

For a few hundred years after a supernova, a cloud of gas and dust can be seen through a telescope.

Different gases are shown in different colours.

KA-BOOOM!

Name: Crab Nebula
Date of supernova: 1054

KER-RASH!

Name: Cassiopeia A
Date of supernova: 1680s

¡GORGEOUS GALAXIES!

All the stars, planets, gas and dust in a galaxy are held together by gravity. Our own Milky Way Galaxy is around 200,000 light years across. It is rotating around its own centre at a speed of about 210 km (130 miles) per second.

WHAT SHAPES ARE GALAXIES?

There are three main shapes of galaxy: spiral, elliptical and irregular:

SUPERLATIVELY SPIRAL

The Whirlpool Galaxy is a spiral, like our Milky Way.

ELEGANTLY ELLIPTICAL

The shape of a slightly squashed ball, Centaurus A is an elliptical galaxy.

INTERESTINGLY IRREGULAR

Like other irregularly shaped galaxies, the Small Magellanic Cloud is a small galaxy that was pulled out of shape by a larger one - in this case the Milky Way!

JUST PLAIN WEIRD

This ring-shaped galaxy, called Hoag's Object, was formed when a small galaxy travelled through the centre of a larger one.

WHAT IS AT THE DARK HEART OF MOST GALAXIES?

Astronomers believe there is a supermassive black hole (see page 20) at the centre of most galaxies. A supermassive black hole has a mass that is millions or billions of times the mass of the Sun. The Milky Way has a black hole with a mass of 10 million Suns at its heart. It is, usually, a quiet black hole, rarely sucking anything inside. It is also at a very safe distance from Earth: 27,200 light years.

I'm feeling ... HUNGRY!

HOW CAN WE SEE INTO THE PAST?

Light travels 300,000 km (186,000 miles) per second. This means that, the further away something is, the longer its light has taken to reach our eyes. If we look at an object 13 billion light years away, we are seeing it as it was 13 billion years ago. Some of the most distant objects in the universe are quasars. These are galaxies with very active supermassive black holes. As gas falls towards the black hole, huge jets of energy are released. Astronomers think that, in the early days of the universe, many galaxies had active black holes, but they have since grown quiet. When we look at a photo of a quasar, we are looking back in time to when the universe was young.

This quasar, 10 billion light years away, is throwing out a jet of energy.

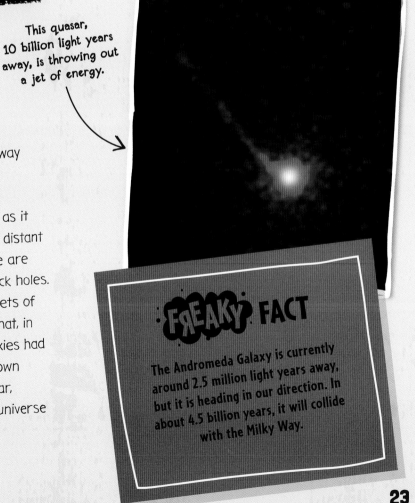

FREAKY FACT

The Andromeda Galaxy is currently around 2.5 million light years away, but it is heading in our direction. In about 4.5 billion years, it will collide with the Milky Way.

UP AND AWAY!

To enter space, a spacecraft must beat the pull of Earth's gravity by travelling faster than 40,000 km (25,000 miles) per hour. By the middle of the 20th century, scientists had built rockets that could fly that terrifyingly fast!

Wheeeee ...!

Vostok 1 was just 2.3 m (7.5 ft) wide.

WHO WAS THE FIRST HUMAN IN SPACE?

In 1961, Russia's brave Yuri Gagarin became the first human in space when his spacecraft, *Vostok 1*, was lifted more than 169 km (105 miles) above Earth by a Vostok-K rocket. As planned, *Vostok 1* separated from its rocket, then made one orbit of Earth. Two years later, Russian Valentina Tereshkova became the first woman in space.

WHO HAS SPENT LONGEST IN SPACE?

The astronaut who spent the longest on a single space mission was Valeri Polyakov, who spent 437 days onboard the Russian space station *Mir* in 1994–95. A space station is a spacecraft that orbits Earth and has room for astronauts to live and carry out experiments. Today, the largest human-made object in space is the International Space Station (ISS), where astronauts from many countries stay for up to a year.

NOT MUCH SPACE STATION

Name: Mir Space Station

In use: 1986–2000

Size: 19 m by 31 m (62 ft by 103 ft)

WILL HUMANS LIVE ON MARS?

The United States, Russian and European space agencies have plans to send astronauts to visit Mars in the next 20 to 30 years. Before humans can actually live there, scientists need to design spacecraft large enough to carry vehicles and materials for building. Since there is no liquid water on Mars, they need to build machines that could gather water contained in the soil. Oxygen for breathing could be made by splitting this water into its two ingredients: oxygen and hydrogen.

I'm thinking of making some improvements to the garden.

SPACIOUS SPACE STATION

SUPER SCIENCE

Astronauts on the ISS carry out experiments into how breathing is affected by gravity. This research will help astronauts to live on the Moon or Mars, which are smaller objects than Earth and so have lower gravity. Their work has also developed a medicine to help asthma sufferers on Earth. Asthma is a condition that causes breathing difficulties.

Name: International Space Station

In use: 2000–present

Size: 73 m by 109 m (240 ft by 358 ft)

ROAMING ROBOTS

Some journeys into space are too dangerous or too long for humans. Instead, we can send robots to do the exploring for us. Robots are machines that are able to carry out tasks on their own.

WHAT DO ROVERS DO ON MARS?

The first rover landed successfully on Mars in 1997. Rovers are robotic wheeled vehicles that travel across a planet or moon. On Mars, rovers collect rock samples, then test to discover what they contain or if there are signs of life. The rovers send information and photos back to Earth as radio waves, taking around 14 minutes to reach us.

SUPER SCIENCE

Space probes and rovers communicate with Earth using the Deep Space Network. This is a group of radio antennas, positioned in the US, Spain and Australia. A radio antenna receives an invisible form of energy that travels as a wave, called a radio wave. By changing the speed and size of the waves, different information can be sent.

WHY DO WE SEND TELESCOPES INTO SPACE?

Telescopes give us images of distant objects that human eyes cannot see well or at all. Telescopes gather light or other, invisible forms of energy given off by objects. On Earth, astronomers position their telescopes on mountaintops, where their views are not spoilt by pollution and light from cities. To get an even better view, some telescopes are sent into space by rockets. Orbiting above Earth's atmosphere, these telescopes pick up energy that is absorbed by the atmosphere and cannot be collected by Earth-based telescopes.

HUBBLE SPACE TELESCOPE

Gathers visible light and ultraviolet

JAMES WEBB SPACE TELESCOPE

Collects infrared (heat) energy from the universe's most distant objects

CHANDRA OBSERVATORY

Detects X-rays

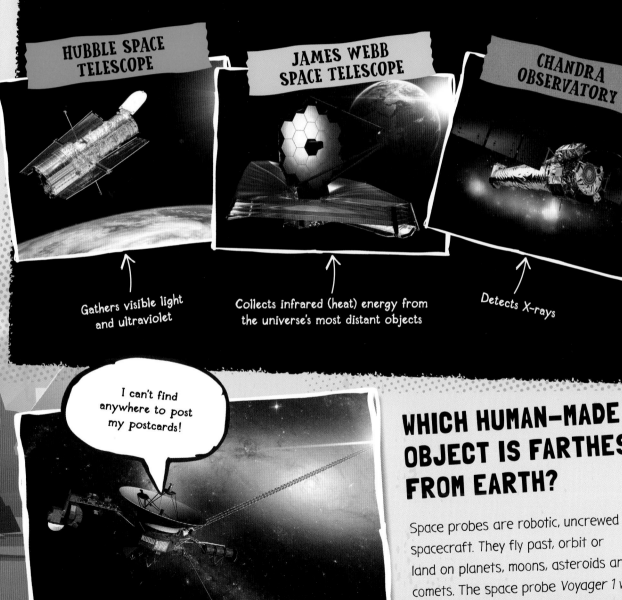

I can't find anywhere to post my postcards!

Voyager 1 left the solar system in 2012.

WHICH HUMAN–MADE OBJECT IS FARTHEST FROM EARTH?

Space probes are robotic, uncrewed spacecraft. They fly past, orbit or land on planets, moons, asteroids and comets. The space probe Voyager 1 was launched in 1977. It is the human-made object that has travelled the farthest, more than 22 billion km (14 billion miles).

ASTONISHING ACTIVITY:
MAKE A BOTTLE ROCKET

Discover how forces make a space rocket shoot upwards! Rather than using rocket fuel, you will use vinegar and bicarbonate of soda to create your force, which is called thrust. You must do this experiment outdoors and with an adult's help.

YOU WILL NEED

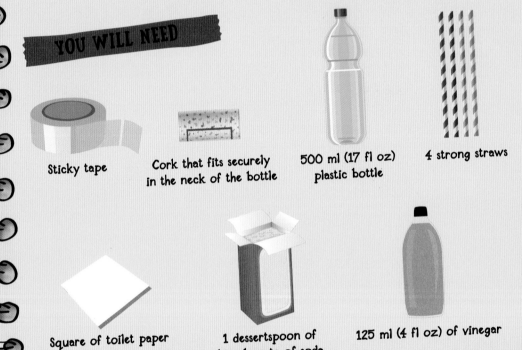

Sticky tape

Cork that fits securely in the neck of the bottle

500 ml (17 fl oz) plastic bottle

4 strong straws

Square of toilet paper

1 dessertspoon of bicarbonate of soda

125 ml (4 fl oz) of vinegar

1 Using sticky tape, secure your four straws to the sides of the bottle so that, when the bottle is turned upside down, it can stand on the straws without tipping over. When resting on its straw legs, the bottle top should be 5 cm (2 in) off the ground.

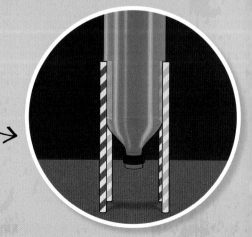

2 Put 1 dessertspoon of bicarbonate of soda on to your square of toilet paper.

3 Fold up the toilet paper square, wrapping the bicarbonate of soda inside to make a packet. Put your packet to one side. (When the packet is dropped into the vinegar, the vinegar and bicarbonate of soda will mix together slowly, delaying your rocket's take-off by a few seconds.)

4 Pour 125 ml (4 fl oz) of vinegar into your plastic bottle, so the bottle is a quarter full.

5 Find a flat patch of ground, away from buildings and power lines, to use as your launch pad. Ask an adult to launch your rocket, while you take at least six large paces backwards, so you are standing at a safe distance.

6 Your adult should drop the packet of bicarbonate of soda into the bottle, then quickly put the cork in the top securely, but not too tightly. Then the adult must place the bottle upside down, resting on its straw legs, and step back five adult paces as fast and safely as they can.

7 What happens to your rocket?

CAPTIVATING CONCLUSION

When vinegar and bicarbonate of soda mix, they release a gas called carbon dioxide. At first, the cork stops the gas from escaping. When the pressure on the cork is too much, the force of the gas pushes out the cork. The contents of the bottle shoot downwards, which makes the bottle fly upwards. This is because, for every force, there is always an equal and opposite reaction. You can demonstrate this in a swimming pool, when you push off from the wall with your feet: the wall exerts an equal and opposite force on your feet, sending you forwards. In a space rocket, the force is created by burning rocket fuel, which make hot gases that shoot out below the rocket. Lift off!

WHOOOOSH…

GLOSSARY

antenna a device for receiving radio waves

asteroid a small rocky object that orbits the Sun

astronomer a scientist who studies planets, stars and space

atmosphere a layer of gases that surround a planet or moon, held by its gravity

atom the smallest particle of any substance that can exist on its own

billion a billion is 1 followed by 9 zeros

black hole a region of space with such powerful gravity that nothing, not even light, can escape its pull

comet an icy object that orbits the Sun on a course that is elliptical

core the inner layer of a planet, moon or star

crust the outer layer of a planet, moon or star

elliptical shaped like an oval

energy the power to do work; energy can take many forms, including light and heat

exoplanet a planet that orbits a star other than our Sun

galaxy a collection of stars, planets, dust and gas, held together by gravity

gravity a force that pulls all objects towards each other; the larger the object, the stronger the pull of its gravity

impact crater a dip in the surface of a planet or moon, caused by being struck by an asteroid or other space object

infrared a form of energy that is invisible to human eyes but can be felt as heat

light year the distance that light travels in a year: 9.46 trillion km (5.88 trillion miles)

mantle the layer of a planet or moon that lies between the crust and the core

mass a measure of the quantity of matter that an object contains; sometimes called 'weight'

moon a large rocky or icy object that is in orbit around a planet

orbit the curved path of a planet or other object around a larger object, such as a star

planet a rocky, icy or gassy object that orbits a star and is large enough for its own gravity to pull it into a ball

radio wave a form of energy that can be used for communication

rocket a vehicle with a powerful engine that lifts spacecraft high above Earth, then is usually discarded

satellite a human-made object that is placed in orbit around Earth or another space object

solar system the Sun and all the planets and other objects in orbit around it

space agency an organization that works on space exploration

space probe a spacecraft without a human crew

star a super-hot ball of gas

theory a set of ideas that try to explain something

trillion a trillion is 1 followed by 12 zeros

ultraviolet a form of energy given off by the Sun that causes human skin to darken

X-ray a form of energy that can pass through many materials

FURTHER READING

BOOKS

Earth and Space (Science in a Flash),
Georgia Amson-Bradshaw (Franklin Watts, 2018)

A Guide to Space,
Kevin Pettman (Wayland, 2020)

Neil Armstrong (Info Buzz),
Izzi Howell (Franklin Watts, 2020)

Space (Maths Problem Solving),
Anita Loughrey (Wayland, 2018)

WEBSITES

Find out more about space and space travel from these websites:

www.spaceplace.nasa.gov/

www.bbc.co.uk/bitesize/topics/zkbbkqt

www.esa.int/kids/en/home

www.sciencemuseum.org.uk/objects-and-stories/space

INDEX

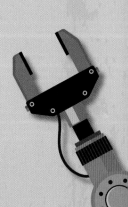

STUPENDOUS AND TREMENDOUS SCIENCE

TITLES IN THE SERIES

Precious Plants
Daring to Be Different
Get to the Root of It
Leave It!
Fierce Flowers
Powerful Pollination
Weird Fruit
Strange Seeds
Killer Plants
Don't Eat Me!
Funky Feeders
Oddly Useful
Astonishing Activity:
Colourful Leaves

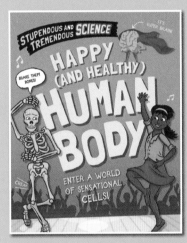

Organised Organs
Super Cells
Got It Covered
Moving Along
Lovely Lungs
Beat It!
Secret Agents
Getting Brainy
Startling Senses
Delicious Digestion
Wonderful Wee
Brilliant Babies
Astonishing Activity:
Getting a Lungful

Your Universe
Extraordinary Earth
Marvellous Moon
Rocky Planets
Watch Out!
Gassy and Giant
Icy and ... Giant
Super Sun
Sparkling Stars
Gorgeous Galaxies
Up and Away!
Roaming Robots
Astonishing Activity:
Make a Bottle Rocket

Eternal Energy
What a Star!
Feeling Hot!
Lovely Light
Shaky Shaky Sound
Crucial Chemical Energy
Moving Along ...
Lots of Potential
Exciting Electricity
Freaky Fossil Fuels
Going Nuclear
Really Renewable
Astonishing Activity:
Static Electricity Race